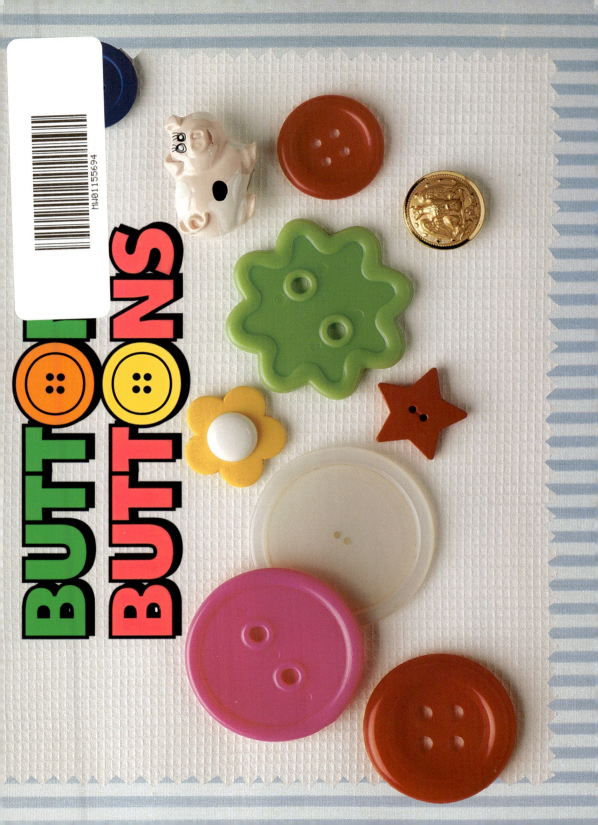

BUTTONS BUTTONS

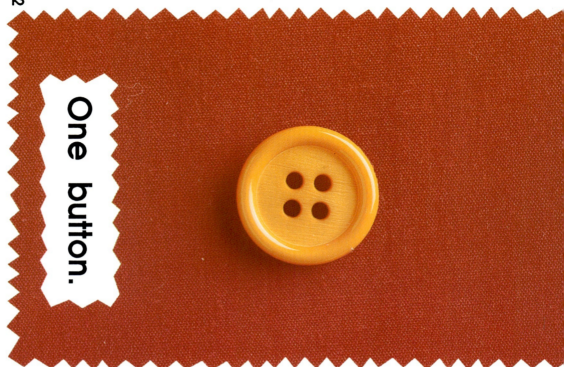

One button.

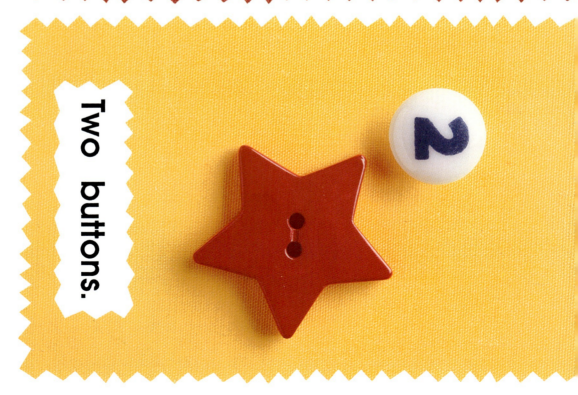

Two buttons.

Blue buttons.

Red buttons.

4

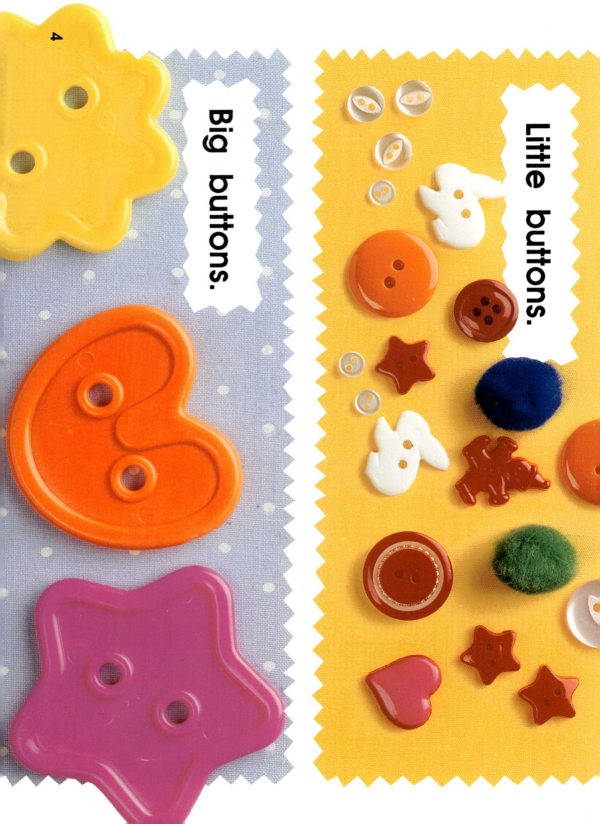

Big buttons.

Little buttons.

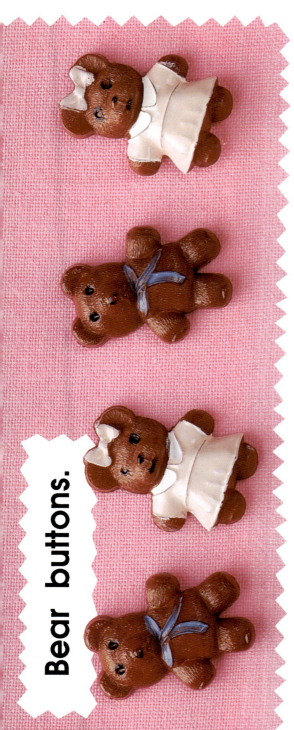

Bear buttons.

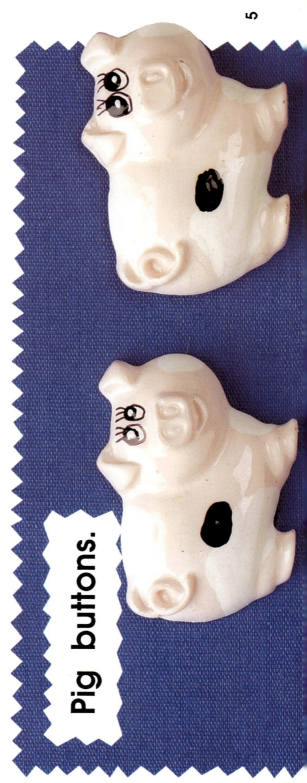

Pig buttons.

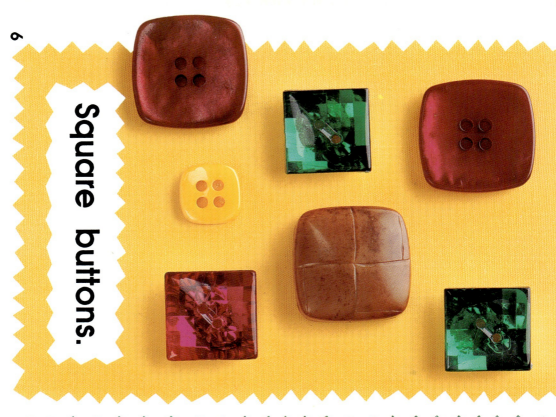

Square buttons.

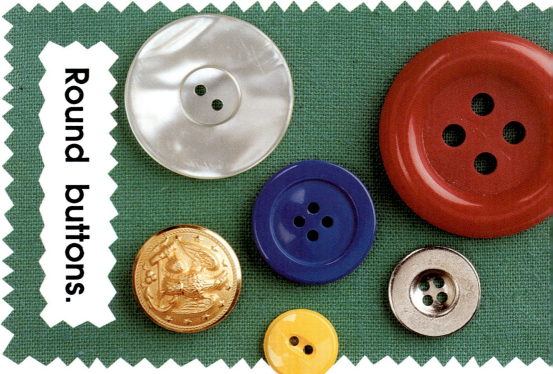

Round buttons.

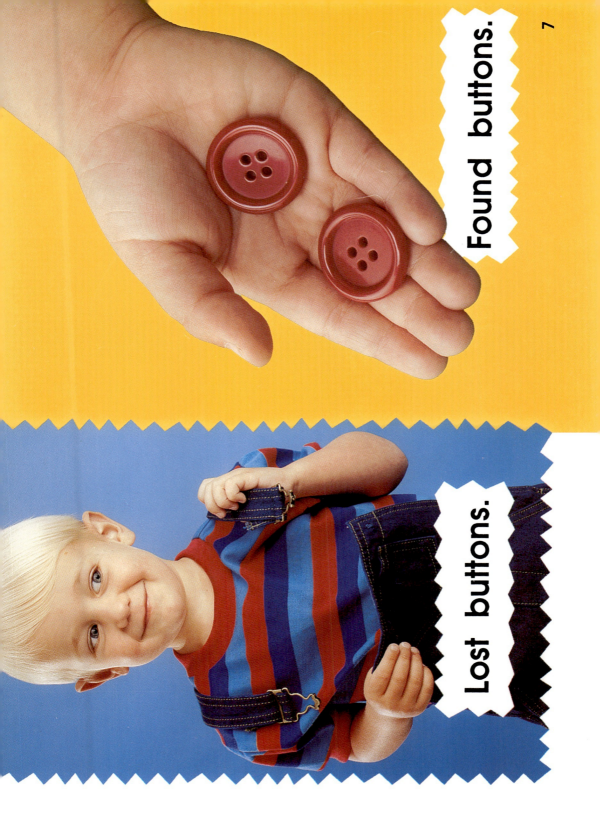

Found buttons.

Lost buttons.

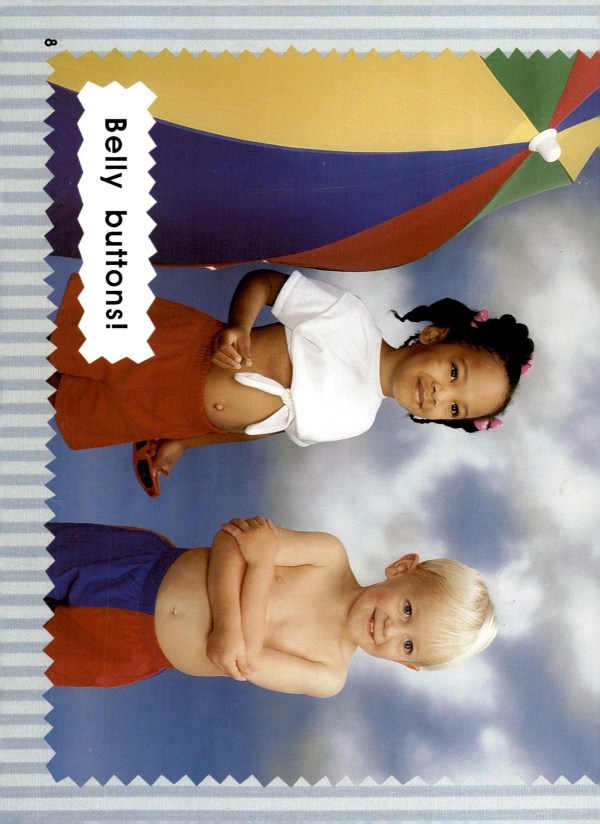

Belly buttons!